GOOD
VIBES
ONLY

Let your
DREAMS
be your
Wings

be
fearless

Be Your
OWN
Sparkle

CREATE
Something
TODAY
EVEN
IF IT
Sucks

COFFEE
Time

be
CREA
TIVE

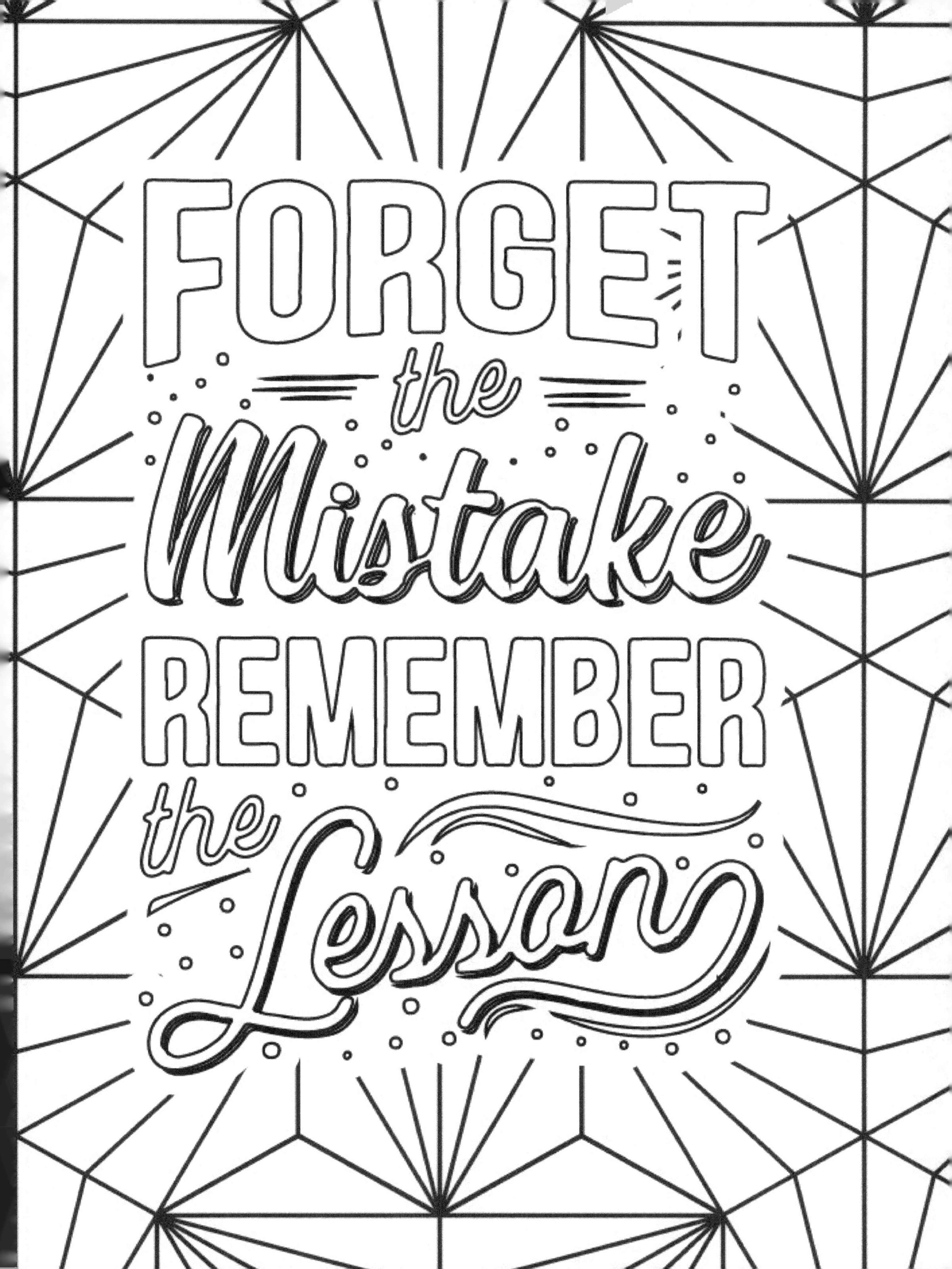

FORGET
the
Mistake
REMEMBER
the
Lesson

focus on
the good

Just
Keep
Pedaling

You
Light Up
my life

Make it Happen SHOCK Everyone

Color
Me
HAPPY

DON'T TELL PEOPLE YOUR DREAMS SHOW TH'EM

live
more
worry
less

plant a seed
OF KINDNESS
reap A
BOUQUET
OF
Happiness

Just
Believe
in your
Dreams

the
BEST
is yet
TO BE

faith
CAN MOVE
mountains

Nature is the Greatest Artist

What you
DO TODAY
CAN
IMPROVE
ALL YOUR
tomorrows

do what
Brings
you
Joy

You Make
me
Smile

life is tough
but so are you

Be The
Best
Version
Of You

BE AS
HAPPY
AS
POSSIBLE

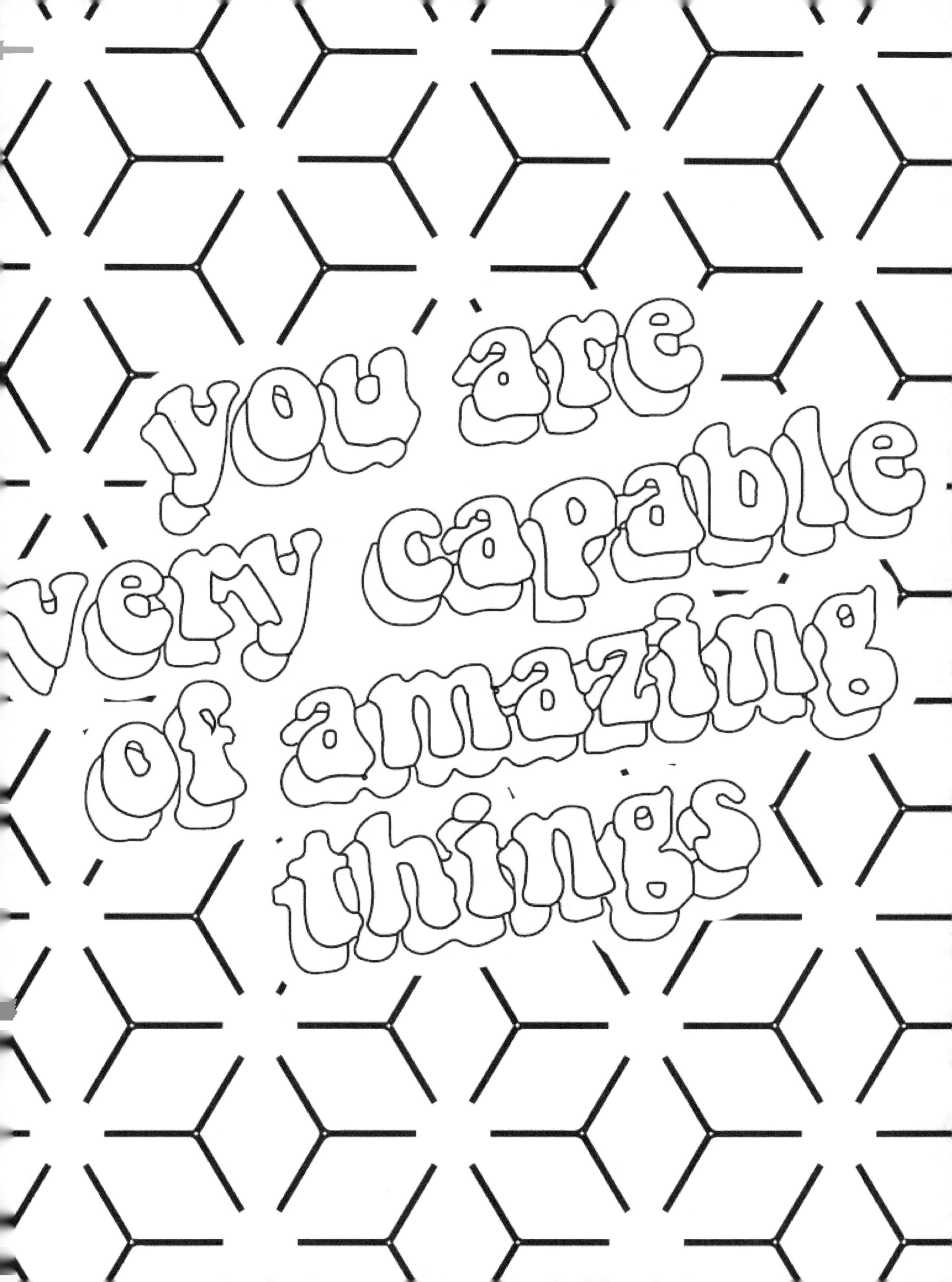
you are
very capable
of amazing
things

Think
HAPPY
Thoughts

Pray More
WORRY LESS

Do Not
GIVE
UP

Creativity
is
INTELLIGENCE
having
FUN

BE
Strong
AND
Courageous

Stay
Humble

STAY
Focused
STAY
Humble

I'm Very
PROUD
OF
me

IF YOU
NEVER GO
YOU'LL NEVER
KNOW

Always Yours

learn
SOMETHING
new
EVERYDAY

IN
Coffee
WE
Trust

BE
Brave
WITH YOUR
Life